W9-CQT-777

**OUR—
SOUTHERN NEIGHBOR
MEXICO**

THE GEOGRAPHY OF MEXICO

COLLEEN MADONNA FLOOD WILLIAMS

Mexico's land possesses an amazing variety of features. This cliff jutting out of the Sea of Cortez provides just one example of the dramatic juxtaposition of different types of geographical elements.

OUR SOUTHERN NEIGHBOR

MEXICO

THE GEOGRAPHY OF MEXICO

COLLEEN MADONNA FLOOD WILLIAMS

Mason Crest Publishers
Philadelphia

To Paul R. Williams and Dillon J. Meehan with love.
Special thanks to Sherry Friedersdorff.

Produced by OTTN Publishing, Stockton, N.J.

Mason Crest Publishers
370 Reed Road
Broomall PA 19008
www.masoncrest.com

3 5 7 9 8 6 4 2

Library of Congress Cataloging-in-Publication Data on file at the Library of Congress

Williams, Colleen Madonna Flood.
  The geography of Mexico / Colleen Madonna Flood Williams.
     p. cm. — (Mexico, our southern neighbor)
Includes bibliographical references and index.
  ISBN 1-59084-075-5
 1. Mexico—Geography--Juvenile literature. I. Title. II. Series.
  F1210.9 .W55 2003
  917.2—dc21
                              2002008932

TABLE OF CONTENTS

OUR
SOUTHERN NEIGHBOR
MEXICO

Roger E. Hernández
Senior Consulting Editor

INTRODUCTION

Mexico is a country in the midst of great change. And what happens in Mexico will have an important impact on the United States, its neighbor to the north.

These changes are being put in place by President Vicente Fox, who was elected in 2000. For the previous 71 years, power had been held by presidents from one single party, known in Spanish as *Partido Revolucionario Institucional* (Institutional Revolutionary Party, or PRI). Some of those presidents have been accused of corruption. President Fox, from a different party called *Partido de Acción Nacional* (National Action Party, or PAN), says he wants to eliminate that corruption. He also wants to have a friendlier relationship with the United States, and for American businesses to increase trade with Mexico. That will create more jobs, he says, and decrease poverty—which in turn will mean fewer Mexicans will find themselves forced to emigrate in search of a better life.

But it would be wrong to think of Mexico as nothing more than a poor country. Mexico has given the world some of its greatest artists and writers. Carlos Fuentes is considered one of the greatest living novelists, and poet-essayist Octavio Paz was awarded the Nobel Prize for Literature in 1990, the most prestigious honor a writer can win. Painters such as Diego Rivera and José Clemente Orozco specialized in murals, huge paintings done on walls that tell of the history of the nation. Another famous Mexican painter, Rufino Tamayo,

7

blended the "cubist" style of modern European painters like Picasso with native folk themes.

Tamayo's paintings in many ways symbolize what Mexico is: A blend of the culture of Europe (more specifically, its Spanish version) and the indigenous cultures that predated the arrival of Columbus.

Those cultures were thriving even 3,000 years ago, when the Olmec people built imposing monuments that survive to this day in what are now the states of Tabasco and Veracruz. Later and further to the south in the Yucatán Peninsula, the Maya civilization flourished. They constructed cities in the midst of the jungle, complete with huge temples, courts in which ball games were played, and highly accurate calendars intricately carved in stone pillars. For some mysterious reason, the Mayans abandoned most of these great centers 1,100 years ago.

The Toltecs, in central Mexico, were the next major civilization. They were followed by the Aztecs. It was the Aztecs who built the city of Tenochitlán in the middle of a lake in what is now Mexico City, with long causeways connecting it to the mainland. By the early 1500s it was one of the largest cities anywhere, with perhaps 200,000 inhabitants.

Then the Spanish came. In 1519, twenty-seven years after Columbus arrived in the Americas, Hernán Cortés landed in Yucatán with just 600 soldiers plus a few cannons and horses. They marched inland, gaining allies as they went along among indigenous peoples who resented being ruled by the Aztecs. Within two years Cortés and the Spaniards ruled Mexico. They had conquered the Aztec Empire and devastated their great capital.

It was in that destruction that modern Mexico was born. The influence of the Aztecs and other indigenous people did not disappear even though untold numbers were killed. But neither can Mexico be recognized today without the Spanish influence.

Spain ruled for three centuries. Then in 1810 Mexicans began a struggle for independence from colonial Spain, much like the United States had fought for its own independence from Great Britain. In 1821 Mexico finally became an independent nation.

The newly born republic faced many difficulties. There was much poverty, especially among descendants of indigenous peoples; most of the wealth and political power was in the hands of a small elite of Spanish ancestry. To make things worse, Mexico lost almost half of its territory to the United States in a war that lasted from 1846 to 1848. Many still resent the loss of territory, which accounts for lingering anti-American sentiments among some Mexicans. The country was later occupied by France, but under national hero Benito Juárez Mexico regained its independence in 1867.

The next turning point in Mexican history came in 1911, when a revolution meant to help the millions of Mexicans stuck in poverty began against dictator Porfirio Díaz. There was violence and fighting until 1929, when Plutarco Elías Calles founded what was to become the *Partido Revolucionario Institucional*. It brought stability as well as economic progress. Yet millions of Mexicans remained in poverty, and as time went on PRI rulers became increasingly corrupt.

It was the desire of the people of Mexico to trust someone other than the candidate of PRI that resulted in the election of Fox. And so this nation of more than 100 million, with its ancient heritage, its diverse mestizo culture, its grinding poverty, and its glorious arts, stands on the brink of a new era. Modern Mexico is seeking a place as the leader of all Latin America, an ally of the United States, and an important voice in global politics. For that to happen, Mexico must narrow the gap between the rich and poor and bring more people in the middle class. It will be interesting to watch as Fox and the Mexican people work to bring their country into the first rank of nations.

HORN OF PLENTY:

THE UNITED MEXICAN STATES

Mexico is a horn of plenty filled with deserts, mountains, *tropical* rain forests, beaches, and plateaus. It is home to the deep sea fishing resorts of Cabo San Lucas, the mountain and jungle bike tours of Troncones, and the desert lava fields of Pinacate. The nation also offers a multitude of ethnic festivals, pre-Columbian ancient ruins, and historic art murals. No wonder this Spanish-speaking country is such a favorite vacation destination for so many Americans. It is truly a land filled with many vastly different sights, sounds, smells, textures, and flavors.

When Americans hear the phrase "south of the border," they think of Mexico, because Mexico is the nation that lies south of the United States' border. Belize and Guatemala border Mexico to the southeast.

The different areas of Mexico are home to a range of weather patterns, from hot and arid to cool and rainy. Mexicans must dress accordingly for the weather conditions, wearing serapes and sombreros to shield them from the elements.

The Gulf of Mexico and the Caribbean Ocean wash along Mexico's eastern shores. The Pacific Ocean and the Gulf of California border the western Mexican coastline.

The Texas-Mexico border follows the winding path of the Río Grande River. However, Mexico is almost three times the size of Texas. It is the third largest country in Latin America. Of the Latin American nations, only Brazil and Argentina are larger.

The country is made up of 32 political regions; 31 of these political regions are states, and the other region is home to the

FAST FACTS

Capital City:	**Mexico City**
Government:	**Democratic Republic**
Official Currency:	**Mexican Peso**
Area:	**760,300 square miles (1,972,500 square kilometers)**
Population:	**100,349,766 as of July 2000**
Ethnic groups:	***mestizo* (Native American-Spanish) 60%, Native American 30%, white 9%, and others 1%**
Religions:	**Roman Catholic 89%, Protestant 6%, and others 5%**
Languages:	**Spanish, Mayan, Nahuatl, and other regional dialects**
Continent:	**North America**
Climate:	**tropical to desert**
Terrain:	**Coastal lowlands, central high plateaus, deserts, and mountains.**
Lowest point:	**sea level at the coast**
Highest point:	**Citlatépetl, 18,696 feet (5,665 meters)**
Natural resources:	**petroleum, silver, copper, gold, lead, zinc, natural gas, timber.**

The varied Mexican landscape offers numerous opportunities for Mexicans to illegally cross the border to the United States. It is difficult for border police to patrol such a large area, and illegal immigrants may attempt to cross the Rio Grande or jump the fence to America. Though thousands of these attempts are hindered by vigilant border police, an unknown number of Mexicans make it into the United States.

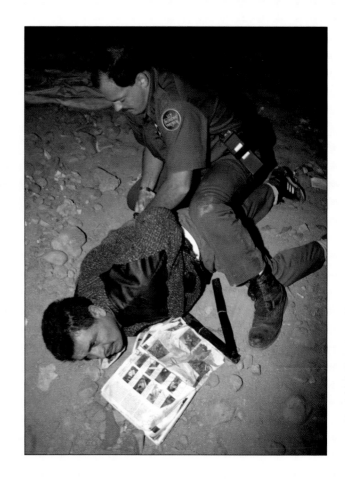

nation's capital, Mexico City. This zone is known as the Federal District.

Mexico City is the capital of Mexico. It is also Mexico's largest city. The crown jewel of the United Mexican States covers an area of 571 square miles (1,479 square kilometers). The population of Mexico City, as of the year 2000, was over 20 million. This makes it one of the largest cities in the world.

Mexico City is also, perhaps, one of the most majestic cities in the world. Mountains surround the city, and great volcanoes stand at its sides. The Pyramid of the Sun and the Pyramid of the Moon are visible

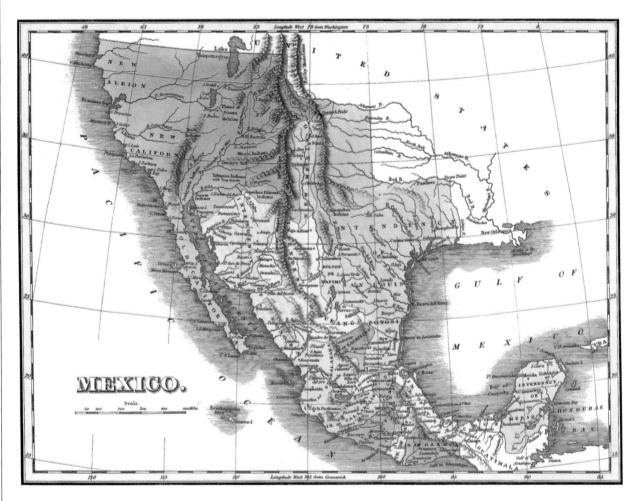

As this 1826 map of Mexico shows, the country was once much larger than it is today, controlling a vast area that is now part of the United States. Though the country's boundaries have changed since then, Mexico still features a great number of varied geographical features. The mountains, rivers, volcanoes, and beaches of Mexico offer a limitless array of sights and experiences.

in the nearby distance. What's more, it is the oldest and the highest city on the North American continent. Over 600 years old, it sits, as if atop a throne, at an elevation of 7,349 feet (2,267 meters). The ruins of an Aztec temple still stand in the center of the city. This busy metropolis is a city with a long, proud history.

Its history begins with the Aztecs who built the ancient foundations of Mexico City on an island in Lake Texcoco over 2,000 years ago. This now crowded modern industrial center was once the center of the Aztec empire. At that time, Mexico City was called Tenochtitlán.

Located in the Valley of Mexico, Mexico City has historically been the center of the nation's population and industrial growth. Nearly one fifth of the entire nation lives in or around

STATE	CAPITAL
1. Aguascalientes	Aguascalientes
2. Baja California	Mexicali
3. Baja California Sur	La Paz
4. Campeche	Campeche
5. Coahuila	Saltillo
6. Colima	Colima
7. Chiapas	Tuxtla Gutierrez
8. Chihuahua	Chihuahua
9. Federal District	
10. Durango	Durango
11. Guanajuato	Guanajuato
12. Guerrero	Chilpancingo
13. Hidalgo	Pachuca
14. Jalisco	Guadalajara
15. Mexico	Toluca
16. Michoacán	Morelia
17. Morelos	Cuernavaca
18. Nayarit	Tepic
19. Nuevo Leon	Monterrey
20. Oaxaca	Oaxaca
21. Puebla	Puebla
22. Queretaro	Queretaro
23. Quintana Roo	Chetumal
24. San Luis Potosi	San Luis Potosi
25. Sinaloa	Culiacan
26. Sonora	Hermosillo
27. Tabasco	Villahermosa
28. Tamaulipas	Ciudad Victoria
29. Tlaxcala	Tlaxcala
30. Veracruz	Xalapa
31. Yucatán	Mérida
32. Zacatecas	Zacatecas

Mexico's beautiful white sand beaches draw thousands of tourists each year, providing an economic boost. Mexico has become an increasingly popular vacation spot for foreigners, especially Americans.

the capital city. Almost every main north-south transportation route runs through the city.

The other 31 political regions of Mexico are home to a great variety of human, plant, and animal life. Differing elevations and climates have created a wide range of **ecosystems**. Even the soil can change dramatically from place to place within Mexico.

Mexico is, indeed, a horn of plenty filled with many different geographical and historical splendors. Deserts cover parts of the nation, while tropical rainforests flourish over others. Volcanoes tower in some areas, while elsewhere lowlands sink slowly toward the seas. Aztec

The ancient people of Mexico glorified nature and their gods through the temples they built. The Pyramid of the Sun, as well as many smaller pyramids, stands in the pre-Columbian city of Teotihuacan.

ruins, once the sites of human sacrifices and other mysterious rituals, stand quietly alongside great Catholic cathedrals.

Mexico is a land of great diversity—but the Mexican people are united. Their government, their history, and their love for this great nation draw them together.

Tall saguaro cacti are silhouetted against the sunset in the Sonoran Desert.
This large desert stretches across Mexico and into the United States as well.

2

HOT, MEDIUM, OR MILD:
THE MANY CLIMATES OF MEXICO

The Tropic of Cancer divides Mexico. It crosses central Mexico and passes through the southern end of Baja California. The part of Mexico that is south of the Tropic of Cancer lies within the earth's tropical climate zone. The part of Mexico that is north of the Tropic of Cancer lies within the earth's **temperate** climate zone.

These two main climate zones, extreme **altitude** changes, and different landscapes work together to create five basic climate areas. Like her spicy **salsas**, Mexico's climate comes in a variety of flavors. At any given moment, somewhere in Mexico, the weather may be red hot, hot, medium, or mild.

The hot land, or *Tierra Caliente,* is the tropical area that falls between sea level and 3,000 feet. The average daily temperature for a tropical city in this area is about 77 degrees Fahrenheit (25 degrees

Although Mexico's rainy season starts in May, the Mexican hurricane season doesn't really step into high gear until June.

Celsius). This area is an enormous **basin** that begins in the state of Jalisco and continues to the state of Guerrero.

One very special part of tropical Mexico is the Lacandona Rain Forest. This lush tropical rain forest is in the eastern area of Chiapas. Over 4,000 kinds of plants grow in this area. Lacandona's wildlife includes the jaguar, harpy eagles, toucans, scarlet and green macaws, and spider and howler monkeys.

The western half of Lacandona is made up of mountain ranges and narrow valleys. The eastern half of the region is low plains, with secluded hills and valleys. The climate is warm and humid. The average annual temperature is above 75 degrees Fahrenheit (about 24 degrees Celsius).

Mexico's central **plateau** and parts of her highlands are at altitudes between 3,000 and 6,000 feet (about 1,000 to 2,000 meters) above sea level. These areas fall into a climate zone called the *Tierra Templada,* or temperate lands. The average

On August 3–4, 1997, the center of Hurricane Guillermo raged less than 700 miles southwest of Cabos San Lucas. This fierce hurricane had winds exceeding 160 miles per hour. Wind gusts exceeded 200 miles per hour. Guillermo created the most powerful winds ever recorded up to that time in the eastern Pacific.

The weather was sunny and warm in Cabos San Lucas on August 3 and 4, 1997. The seas swelled to 12 feet, however. Waves came crashing in from the storm center over 600 miles away. They ravaged the beaches. Between Cabos San Lucas and San Jose del Cabo, the force of the storm was incredible. Waves from the Sea of Cortez crashed into beachfront resorts. Flooding damaged condominiums and homes. Rogue waves swept at least two sightseers to their deaths.

Guillermo's fury was so great that eight-foot breakers crashed into the beaches of Los Angeles. (Los Angeles was more than 1,500 miles away from the storm!)

The white, wind-blown sand of the Chihuahuan Desert stretches into the distance. Though the land is dry and the air hot, some plants are able to thrive.

The Nevado de Toluca volcano rises almost 15,000 feet into the sky. The volcano is no longer active; today it is surrounded by forest.

temperatures of this region fall between 60 to 72 degrees Fahrenheit (about 15 to 22 degrees Celsius).

Tierra Fría means the cold land. This climate zone climbs from 6,000 feet to as high as 11,000 feet (about 2,000 to almost 3,000 meters). **Alpine pastures** cover the tops of these altitudes.

Tierra Helada is the Spanish way of saying "the frozen land." This is the name given to the permanent snow line. The frozen land of central Mexico is found at altitudes of 13,000 to 14,000 feet (about 4,000 meters).

Mexico's desert climate is its driest and hottest climate. Most of the largest desert in North America lies south of the border. The Chihuahuan Desert covers more than 200,000 square miles, stretching from just south of Albuquerque, New Mexico, to the state of Zacatecas in Mexico.

In the Chihuahuan Desert, winters are short. For brief periods, however, the temperatures may fall below freezing. Summer temperatures are blistering. The high temperatures are often over 100 degrees (about 38 degrees Celsius). Most of the area receives less than 10 inches of rainfall yearly.

Another North American desert, the Sonoran Desert, covers approximately 120,000 square miles. It covers much of

Guadalajara's climate is typical of the south-central highlands. This Tierra Templada city has a spring-like climate year round. Guadalajara is Mexico's second largest city.

A city of festivals, mariachi bands, and artisans, Guadalajara's lovely weather contributes to its happy atmosphere. Its high temperatures average around 80 degrees Fahrenheit (about 27 degrees Celsius), while its lows average around 53 degrees Fahrenheit (about 12 degrees Celsius). With weather like that, no wonder the street bands are always playing!

Mexico City, the capital of Mexico, as seen at twilight. One of the largest and most developed cities in Mexico, it is an important social and cultural center.

southwestern Arizona and southeastern California. It also extends into most of Baja California and the western half of the state of Sonora, Mexico.

The Sonoran Desert has temperatures of 50 to 60 degrees Fahrenheit (10 to 15 degrees Celsius) even in the winter. In the summer, its temperatures can soar to well above 100 degrees Fahrenheit. Fewer than 10 inches of rainfall fall here yearly.

Although little rain falls in Mexico's desert areas, the Mexican rains divide the rest of the country's year into two main seasons. Summer is Mexico's rainy season, lasting from May to October. During this time, there are daily showers throughout most of the country. October to May marks the winter season for most Mexicans, and during the winter, most of the country is subjected to the dry season. Water becomes a precious commodity for many Mexican farmers during these months. Only the northwestern part of Baja California gets most of its rainfall during the winter.

Winter is also hurricane season for the coastal areas of Mexico. Mexico's Baja California peninsula becomes increasingly vulnerable to hurricanes

Mexico City's climate is a product of both the city's latitude, which is south of the Tropic of Cancer, and its elevation of 7,347 feet (about 2,226 meters). The city is located in a tropical climatic zone. However, its extremely high altitude contributes to its moderate climate. The average annual temperature is about 61 degrees Fahrenheit (16 degrees Celsius). The coldest month of the year is January, when the average ranges from as low as 44 degrees Fahrenheit to 70 degrees Fahrenheit (about 7 to 21 degrees Celsius). The warmest month is generally May, when the temperatures range from 54 to 78 degrees Fahrenheit (12 to 25 degrees Celsius).

Cabo San Lucas in Baja California Sur is an important port; it receives imported goods, as well as cruise ships full of tourists. Though Mexico's economy is not always stable, it is helped by foreign money through those two avenues.

beginning in July. Cabo San Lucas and La Paz are also most likely to be hit by hurricanes during July. The biggest hurricane danger for the eastern Mexican coast begins in August and lasts through October. The odds of a hurricane striking Mexico's west coast are at their highest in September.

Several hurricanes per year whirl along the Caribbean and Gulf of Mexico coastline. These storms bring high winds, heavy rain, widespread damage, and sometimes loss of life. Hurricane Hugo passed directly over Cancún in September 1989. Hugo's high winds wreaked havoc on the hotels along Cancún's beaches.

Eight years later, Hurricane Pauline caused about 300 deaths when Pauline hit with a terribly destructive force. The hurricane struck the Pacific coastal states of Guerrero and Oaxaca during October of 1997.

Hurricanes along the Gulf and the Caribbean coasts are not the only natural disasters that plague Mexico. The country experiences *tsunamis* along the Pacific coast and destructive earthquakes in the center and south. Volcanic eruptions are always a threat throughout the Trans-Mexican Volcanic Belt. Mexico is an important part of the Pacific's "Ring of Fire," a circle of active volcanoes.

From the heights of the frozen land to the sands of her hot, dry Chihuahuan Desert, Mexico is a land of extremes. At one moment, it is cool and serene. The next moment, it may be hot and turbulent. Its climate, tropical storms, hurricanes, tsunamis, earthquakes, and volcanic eruptions all join in to create the spicy mixture that is Mexico.

This portion of the Sierra Madre Oriental is protected as a national park.
Here, tectonic forces thrust up limestone strata to nearly vertical angles.

3

TOPOGRAPHY:
LIKE A SOMBRERO

Like a **sombrero**, all sides of the Mexican mainland slope upward toward the central region. The central region is an elevated plain surrounded by mountains. The Mexican *altiplano*, or central plain, runs between the Eastern and Western Sierra Madre Mountain chains. Altiplano means "high plain."

A plain is a broad, flat, or gently rolling area. Plains are usually low in elevation, but most of Mexico's plains are high plains or plateaus. A plateau is flat highland area, often with one steep face. Basically, a plateau is an elevated plain.

High plateaus and mountains cover two thirds of the country. Still, Mexico manages to cling to its diversity. The bright beautiful sombrero that is Mexico's mainland is embroidered with a distinctive patchwork of earth-toned deserts, jewel-painted tropical forests, water-colored coastlines, and grassy green valleys.

Mexico has three major mountain ranges and one volcanic belt. The mountain ranges are all part of the Sierra Madre Mountains—the

Eastern Sierra Madres, or Sierra Madre Orientals; the Western Sierra Madres, or Sierra Madre Occidentals; and the Southern Sierra Madres, or the Sierra Madres del Sur. The Trans-Mexican Volcanic Belt runs from east to west in southern Mexico.

The Western Sierra Madre Range starts beneath the Arizona border. The mountains then run south to the Santiago River. Here they turn into the Trans-Mexican Volcanic Belt. The belt runs east and west. The northwest coastal plain is the lowland area between the Western Sierra Madre and the Gulf of California. The Western Sierra Madre Mountains average 7,425 feet (2,250 meters) in elevation, with peaks reaching almost 10,000 feet (3,000 meters).

The Eastern Sierra Madre Mountains start at the Big Bend region of the Texas-Mexico border. The range runs southward. It, too, meets the Trans-Mexican Volcanic Belt in the South. The northeast coastal plain sprawls from east of the Eastern Sierra Madre to the Gulf of Mexico. The average elevation of the Sierra Madre Oriental is 7,260 feet (2,200 meters), with some peaks at nearly 10,000 feet (3,000 meters).

There is one other major mountain range in the northern half of Mexico. The Sierra de la Giganta runs from the United States border to the southern end of the Baja Peninsula. Its peaks range in altitude from 7,260 feet in the north to only 825 feet (250 meters). This range plunges into the Sea of Cortez near La Paz in the south. Narrow lowlands are found to the east and west of these mountains.

The Trans-Mexican Volcanic Belt is 558 miles (900 kilometers) long and 80 miles (130 kilometers) wide. It stretches from the Pacific Ocean to the Gulf of Mexico. The belt starts at the Río Grande de Santiago. From there,

The agave plant is capable of growing in somewhat arid conditions. Its spiny leaves are sometimes cultivated for their fiber or sap.

it spreads south to Colima, and from Colima, the belt runs east to the center of the state of Veracruz.

The belt contains Mexico's highest volcanic peaks; three peaks are higher than 1,500 feet (5,000 meters). Pico de Orizaba, found in the belt, is the third highest mountain in North America. Pico de Orizaba is 18,406 feet high (5,610 meters). The belt's other two great peaks are Popocatépetl and Iztaccíhuatl.

Whether from volcanoes or earthquakes, like a jumping bean, Mexico is almost always in motion. This is because Mexico sits right on top of three large **tectonic plates**. These plates are called the American, Caribbean, and the Cocos. The motion of these plates causes earthquakes and volcanic activity. The Baja California Peninsula is on the Pacific Plate. Earthquakes in this region pulled the Baja California Peninsula away from the coast. This created the Gulf of California.

The Rio Grande River forms part of the boundary between the United States and Mexico. It flows 1,885 miles, from the San Juan Mountains in Colorado to the Gulf of Mexico.

Along Mexico's southern coast ambles the Sierra Madre del Sur. The southern Sierra Madres stretch from the southwestern part of the Trans-Mexican Volcanic Belt to the Isthmus of Tehuantepec. (An isthmus is a piece of land that joins two larger pieces of land together.) Mountains in this range average more than 6,000 feet (2,000 meters) in elevation.

Pico de Orizaba is the starting point for the Sierra Madre de Oaxaca. This range ends at the Isthmus of Tehuantepec. Summits in the Sierra Madre de Oaxaca average more than 8,000 feet (2,500 meters) in elevation, with some mountains exceeding 10,000 feet.

The Sierra Madre de Chiapas run along the Pacific Coast, south of the Isthmus of Tehuantepec. These mountains stretch from the Oaxaca-Chiapas border to the Mexico-Guatemala border. The average height of the mountains in this range is only 5,000 feet (1,500 meters). Volcán de Tacuma towers above most of the range, reaching over 4,000 meters in height.

Much of Mexico's land may be mountainous, but most of Mexico's population lives on its central plateau. This area of Mexico is in between the Western Sierra Madre and the Eastern Sierra Madre mountain ranges. The plateau generally ranges in elevation from about 3,000 feet (900 meters) in its northern regions to about 8,000 feet (about 2,400 meters) in the south.

Think of Mexico's two peninsulas as the strings that would secure the sombrero around the wearer's neck. The Baja California Peninsula of northwestern Mexico is directly south of California. It contains the states of Baja California Norte and Baja California Sur. The peninsula separates the Gulf of California from the Pacific Ocean. (The Gulf of California is also known as the Sea of Cortez.) The Yucatán Peninsula juts out to the northeast from the Isthmus of Tehuantepec. It extends into the Gulf of Mexico.

The Baja Peninsula is about 760 miles (about 1,200 kilometers) long. It varies in width from 30 to 150 miles (48 to 241 kilometers). Baja California Norte, with its capital city of Mexicali, is in the north. Baja California Sur, with its capital city of La Paz, is in the south.

The Baja California Peninsula has three main mountain ranges. The Sierra de la Giganta Mountains run along the eastern coast of the state of Baja California Sur, with peaks more than 10,000 feet (3,000 meters) above sea level. The Sierra de San Boria Mountains are found in the southern region of Baja California Norte. The Sierra de San Pedro Martir are found in the northern region of Baja California Norte.

The Yucatán Peninsula is made up of flat lowlands. The northwestern peninsula is dry and brushy, while in the south, where rainfall is abundant, the peninsula is covered by tropical rain forests.

The narrowest part of Mexico, between the gulfs of Campeche and Tehuantepec, is the Isthmus of Tehuantepec. This isthmus is approximately 130 miles wide at its narrowest point. The Isthmus of Tehuantepec is all that separates the Gulf of Mexico from the Pacific Ocean along this section of Mexico.

The Isthmus of Tehuantepec is a gently sloped lowland region. The northern side of the isthmus is wet, swampy, and thickly covered with jungle. Its southern Pacific slopes are drier. The lowest point of the isthmus is at about 754 feet (230 meters) above sea level.

Mexico has almost 150 rivers. Most of these rivers drain into the Pacific Ocean. Few of them flow into the Gulf of Mexico or the Caribbean Sea. Water is a precious commodity in many areas, because of the locations of the major rivers.

Mexico has five major rivers. All five of these rivers flow into the Gulf of Mexico. Northern and central Mexico, home to almost 60 percent of Mexico's population, have less than 10 percent of the country's water resources.

The Grijalva River begins in Guatemala, then flows through the state of Chiapas, and empties into the Gulf of Mexico near Villahermosa. It is one of Mexico's few rivers that are **navigable**, but small boats can travel on only a few areas of the river.

The Usumacinta River also starts in Guatemala. It travels east through Chiapas, and then meets and joins the Grijalva River near the Gulf of Mexico.

The Infiernillo Dam is on the Balsas River southwest of Mexico City. This dam helps to contain one of the largest water *reservoirs* in the country. It runs along the border between the states of Guerrero and Michoacán.

The Papaloapan River originates in the mountains north of the Isthmus of Tehuantepec and then flows east. The Papaloapan River empties into the Gulf of Mexico near Coatzacoalcos.

Two rivers form the largest and most important river system in Mexico. The Grande de Santiago and Lerma Rivers flow into and out of Lake Chapala. The Lerma begins in the Western Sierra Madre Mountains and flows into Lake Chapala, while the Grande de Santiago flows out of the Lake Chapala and empties into the Pacific Ocean. The Grande de Santiago serves as a major source of *hydroelectric* power.

The Río Grande winds along the entire Texas-Mexico border. Farmers in both the United States and the United Mexican States have come to depend upon the Río Grande. It is a major source of water for irrigation projects in both Texas and Mexico.

Lakes and lagoons are very important in Mexico. Lakes are inland bodies of water that do not touch the sea. Lagoons are found along the coasts, and are separated from the sea by only a strip of land. Like Mexico's rivers, their water is used for agriculture irrigation projects. Without them, Mexico's farmers would have very little farming success. Mexico does not have a large number of lagoons and lakes, however. The largest lakes in the Republic of Mexico are Lakes Chapala, Cuitzeo, and Pátzcuaro. The largest lagoons are the lagoons of Tamiahua and Términos.

Lake Chapala is south of the city of Guadalajara. It is the largest lake in the country, about 50 miles (80 kilometers) long and about 8 miles (13 kilometers) at its widest point. Lake Xochimilco is south of Mexico City in the Valley of Mexico. It is one of the most famous lakes in all of Mexico.

Mexico has three major gulfs. A gulf is part of a sea or ocean that reaches into the land. It is usually larger than a bay. The Gulf of Mexico is found on the eastern coast of Mexico. The Gulf of California, or the Sea of Cortez, is between the Baja Peninsula and the western coast of mainland Mexico. The Gulf of Tehuantepec is located along the southwestern Mexico along the western coast of the Isthmus of Tehuantepec.

Mexico has many bays along its coastlines. A bay is also a part of a body of salt water that reaches inland, but it is generally smaller in size than a gulf. The Bay of Sebastian Vizcaino lies along the west of the Baja California Peninsula. The Island of Cedros is located between it and the Pacific Ocean. Within the Gulf of California, along the eastern coast of the Baja Peninsula, are the Bay of Coyote, the Bay of Los Angeles, and the Bay of Santa Ana. Along

Lake Xochimilco is known for its floating gardens. The lake is just south of Mexico City. The Aztecs piled layers of mud and marsh plants into the lake to create small islands. They then planted flowers and plants on these little islands (known as chinampas). The islands do not really float, although they look as if they do. The chinampas of Lake Xochimilco still provide the citizens of Mexico City with fresh flowers and vegetables to this day.

Deserted fishing boats float in Lake Chapala. Fishing is an important source of revenue and food for some Mexican families.

the western coast of mainland Mexico, within the Gulf of California, are the Bay of Adair, the Bay of Tepoca, and the Bay of Santa Maria.

The Yucatán Peninsula has several bays along the Caribbean Ocean. The bays of Calderitas, Espiritu Santo, and the Ascension extend inland from the Caribbean to the Yucatán Peninsula. Along the Yucatán's Gulf of Mexico coastline are a number of lagoons.

Mexico's coastline is one of the longest in the world. It is about 5,800 miles long (9,330 kilometers). Mexico's western coast is almost twice the length of its eastern coast.

Veracruz, Tampico, and Coatzacoalcos are the major eastern ports. They are all on the Gulf of Mexico. Acapulco, Manzanillo, Mazatlán, and Salina Cruz are the major ports in the west. These ports are along the North Pacific Ocean.

Mexico's many islands are as diverse as the different regions of its mainland. Two important islands in the Gulf of California are Angel de la Guarda (Island of the Guardian Angel) and Tiburon (Shark Island). Cozumel and the Island of Women are two important islands in the Gulf of Mexico. The Island of Guadalupe is in the Pacific Ocean.

The Island of Guadalupe is Mexico's westernmost island off Baja California. It is approximately 160 miles (258 kilometers) from shore. This is a volcanic oceanic island. It is about 22 miles (35 kilometers) long and about 4 to 6 miles (7 to 10 kilometers) wide. There is very little fresh water on the island, and it is particularly scarce at the higher altitudes of the island. The island reaches elevations of 4,200 feet (1,280 meters) at its northern end.

Cozumel is Mexico's largest inhabited island. The island is located just 12 miles (19 kilometers) off the Yucatán Coast. It is 29 miles (47 kilometers) long and 10 miles (15 kilometers) wide. Cozumel is actually divided into a coastal city and an island city.

A dense jungle covers Cozumel's interior, while its beaches are covered with ivory white sands. Cozumel's shore is home to one of the most dramatic collections of **coral reefs** in the Gulf of Mexico.

The Isla Mujeres, or the Island of Women, is located just eight miles across the Bahia de Mujeres (Bay of Women) from Cancún. The Island of Women is only 5 miles (8 kilometers) long and half a mile wide. The average temperature is 80 degrees Fahrenheit (27 degrees Celsius). The island's terrain is flat, with beaches on all sides.

The Island of the Guardian Angel and Shark Island divide the Gulf of California into two sections. Shark Island is an island off the coast of Sonora. It is the largest island in all of Mexico, approximately 31 miles (50 kilometers) long and 15.5 miles (25 kilometers) wide), with a surface area of about 480 square miles (1,208 square kilometers). It is home to two low mountain ranges that reach heights of up to 400 feet (1,315 meters) above sea level.

The Island of the Guardian Angel is the second largest island in the Gulf of California. It is 43 miles (70 kilometers) long and about 12 miles (20 kilometers) at its widest, and its surface area is roughly 533 square miles (about 895 square kilometers). It is made up of a steep mountain range so that the island literally rises from the

> The second largest coral reef in the world starts at Cozumel. It is the exotic black coral reef called Palancar Reef. Jacques Costeau is credited with discovering it.

An excursion boat for tourists is anchored along the shore near Cozumel. The tourism industry has created new jobs in Mexico, as people come from all over the world to enjoy the country's beautiful scenery.

seabed. The mountains of Guardian Angel Island reach a maximum height of about 1,315 feet (400 meters) at the north end of the island.

In the northwest of Mexico, including much of the Baja Peninsula, lies the Sonoran Desert. This desert is as diverse as the rest of Mexico. In places, it is perhaps the most fertile **badland** of them all. In others, it is the harshest desert climate in North America.

The Grand Desert region of the Sonoran Desert is located in Mexico to the east of the Colorado River. It is home to the harshest, sandiest, most wind-blown desert terrain. The region of the Sonoran Desert that is found within the state of Sonora has a longer, wetter summer rainy season with a drier winter. The Sonoran Desert on Baja is often called the Vizcaino Desert.

> Cozumel is warm all year long, with an average temperature of 81 degrees Fahrenheit (27 degrees Celsius). Heavy rains start in June and go on through October.

The Chihuahuan Desert is the easternmost and southernmost of the four North American deserts: the Great Basin Desert, the Sonoran Desert, the Mojave Desert, and the Chihuahuan Desert. Much of the Chihuahuan Desert lies within the boundaries of the Mexican Plateau. It is bounded on the west by the Sierra Madre Occidental and on the east by the Sierra Madre Oriental, with its southern boundary in Zacatecas. It extends from Mexico into southeastern Arizona, southern New Mexico, and Trans-Pecos Texas.

The North Caineville Mesa dominates the landscape in the Mexican desert. The Mesa can be seen along the Outlaw Trail, a rough route that runs from northern Montana to Mexico.

THE REGIONS OF MEXICO

The majority of Mexicans live, work, and play on the Mexican Plateau. The plateau can be divided into two major parts: the Northern Plateau and the Central Plateau.

The Northern Region of the Central Plateau begins near the U.S. border. It ends near San Luis Potosí. In this dryer part of the Mexican Plateau, few people live. Those who do, live around the areas that lend themselves to irrigation.

In the Salado River valley of the Northern Plateau, wheat is grown. In its Laguna Basin area, much of Mexico's cotton is grown. Other crops include corn (maize), beans, and alfalfa, and large areas of the more arid land are utilized as rangeland for cattle. There are few permanent streams in this region.

The Central Plateau is often called the "Mexican Heartland." This is because the Central Plateau has some of Mexico's most fertile farmland. The temperate climate combined with the fairly abundant rainfall and rich volcanic soils make this region very good for farming.

The Central Plateau is used for raising cattle in some of its drier areas to the north. The major crops raised in this region are corn, beans, wheat, and sugarcane. There are sugar refineries and grain mills in Guadalajara.

The Central Plateau is home to many important Mexican industries, such as textiles, cement, and chemicals. The major cities within the Central Plateau are Mexico City, Guadalajara, León, Queretaro, and Pachuca. These cities have flourished for many years around the fertile farmlands and industry-friendly landscape of the Central Plateau.

The states of Coahuila, Chihuahua, and Nuevo Leon make up the mountainous northern region of Mexico. Coahuila's capital is Saltillo. It is about 530 feet (1,748 meters) above sea level. This state is famous for its brightly colored handwoven *serapes*.

Monterrey, the capital city of Nuevo León, is famous for being the third largest city in Mexico, as well as a major center of industry. Twenty-five percent of Mexico's manufactured goods are made in and around this city.

Chihuahua City is the capital of Mexico's largest state. Birthplace of the Chihuahua dog, this state is also home to Mexico's large sect of Mennonites. Chihuahua is the state where Mexico's Copper Canyon and the Basaseachi Falls can be found.

Chihuahua is home to the Sierra Tarahumara Indians. An estimated 50,000 Tarahumara still live in small shacks and caves deep within the Sierra Madres and the Copper Canyon. The Tarahumara live as traditionally as possible, shunning the modern technology that most Mexicans have come to take for granted. Their main diet consists of corn tortillas, potatoes, beans, and squash. Their religion is a mix of traditional Indian practices and those brought to them by the Catholic missionaries. The Tarahumara worship the sun and the moon, as well as Jesus Christ, the Christian God, and the Catholic saints.

The Canyon de Sumidero cuts through the Mexican state of Chiapas. Mexico's varied landscape features countless natural land formations.

The Baja California Peninsula starts in the far northwest of the country. It stretches southeast 800 miles (1,290 kilometers) from its U.S. border. The Baja California Peninsula is dry and mountainous, while its coastal plain is very narrow. U.S. tourists visit coastal resorts along the northern Gulf of California and on the Pacific Ocean. The rest of the peninsula is only sparsely inhabited. The Baja Peninsula is home to the states of Baja California Norte and Baja California Sur.

The Gulf Coast plain lies between the Eastern Sierra Madre and the Gulf of Mexico. The coast is made up mainly of swampland and lagoons. Its northern region is dry. In the south, are tropical forests. The southern part of the Gulf Coast Plain, where there is much more rain, is home to some fertile farming lands.

Veracruz, Mexico's most important port, is located in this region. Many of Mexico's oil finds have taken place in this area. Veracruz is

Fertile croplands stretch across the mountains of Mexico. Agriculture remains an important industry in Mexico, where it keeps the demand for imported goods at a reasonable level.

also a favorite vacation destination for many Mexicans. As a result, the people of Veracruz are chiefly employed by the tourist and oil industries. They are known throughout Mexico for their love of **Mardi Gras** and music. Veracruz is said to be the home of the music called "La Bamba." Veracruz is also known to celebrate Mardi Gras with a zest that is rivaled only by that of New Orleans.

The Pacific Lowlands lie between the Western Sierra Madre and the Pacific Ocean. The northern regions are irrigated and used for farming. To the south of Manzanillo, they are bordered by the Sierra Madre del Sur. Mazatlán, Puerto Vallarta, and Manzanillo are three of the important cities found along the Pacific lowland coast.

Many of the people in and around the city of Mazatlán are fishermen, farmers, artisans, and tourist service workers. Mazatlán is also home to Mexico's largest shrimp fleet. The surrounding area farms produce melons, tomatoes, cantaloupes, wheat, and cotton.

The artisans of Concordia, a town 30 miles (48 kilometers) southeast of Mazatlán, produce furniture and pottery. Concordia is proud of its furniture-making tradition. The city center is decorated with an oversized rocking chair in honor of the town's furniture makers.

Oaxaca, Chiapas, and Tabasco are the major Mexican states of the tropical south. The rugged southern state of Oaxaca is only 150 miles (242 kilometers) distant from Mexico City. With the mountains as a barrier to the capital city, however, Oaxaca seems like an entire world away from modern Mexico City. Life is lived more leisurely in Oaxaca than it is in Mexico City, and the population is much smaller. The citizens of Oaxaca are artists, farmers, and weavers. There is no commercial industry or big business here. Although the landscape is rocky and dry, Oaxaca is home to a large Indian population. These Indians are said to produce the finest handicrafts in all of Mexico.

Oaxaca the city is a popular destination for tourists. Thriving village markets surround the city. It is also close to some of Mexico's most spectacular pre-Hispanic Indian ruins. Monte Albán and Yagul are both found within the borders of Oaxaca's Central Valley.

Tabasco is a region of equatorial rainforests. Many rivers run through the state on their way to the Gulf of Mexico. Petroleum and other mineral deposits have led to a chemical industrial boom here. It is a very wealthy state, but Tabasco, homeland of the ancient Olmecs, tends to be sparsely populated. The only heavily populated area is the city of Villahermosa. On the banks of the Grijalva River, this boomtown is famous for its extreme tropical heat and humidity. The ruins of the

48

ancient Olmecs' Comalcalco are close to this city.

Directly south of Tabasco is the poorer state of Chiapas. Although this state faces serious economic struggles, it is nevertheless rich with tremendous diversity. For instance, Chiapas is covered with many volcanic mountains. At the center of Chiapas is San Cristobál de Las Casas, a colonial town seated in the midst of a collection of traditional Indian villages. To the north, the Chiapan rainforest wraps itself around many Mayan ruins. The Agua Azul waterfalls of this region rank among Mexico's most spectacular sights, and the El Triunfo cloud forest in Chiapas dwells beneath an almost constant cloud cover. Combine almost constant rainfall with the cloud cover, and this becomes one of Mexico's wettest and greenest areas. The cloud forest is an ideal habitat for Mexico's quetzal bird, a bird with green tail feathers that reach up to two feet long.

The Yucatán Peninsula is a flat, low-lying region. It reaches northeast from the Isthmus of Tehuantepec into the Gulf of Mexico. Natural *sinkholes* that

Tamahumara Indian women gather in a town plaza in Mexico. The women wear serapes, which are often brilliantly colored wraps.

speckle the landscape of the northern Yucatán were once its only source of water. The important international tourist center of Cancún is located along the eastern coast of the Yucatán.

The northwestern region of the Yucatán Peninsula is dry and brushy. It supports very little farming. In the south, however, rainfall is plentiful. The southern Yucatán Peninsula is covered with tropical rain forests.

The three states that make up the Yucatán Peninsula are Campeche, Yucatán, and Quintana Roo. The people of this region are called Yucatecos. Many Yucatecos are descendants of the Mayan Indians who lived in Yucatán hundreds of years before the Spaniards arrived. A great majority of the Yucatecos are farmers.

Northern Yucatán is an important henequen farming region. Henequen is used to make twine and rope. Other crops grown on the Yucatán Peninsula include *cacao*, *chicle*, coffee, corn, cotton, sugar cane, and tobacco. Cacao is used to make chocolate. Chicle is used to make chewing gum.

Four young Mexican girls watch the skyline in Chihuahua City. Although Mexico's economy has been gradually improving over the years, the cities are home to many impoverished families.

The Popocatépetl volcano lets out a plume of smoke in Puebla, Mexico. In December 2000, the volcano, which has been active for the past six years, spewed ash 11.2 miles into the sky.

NATIONAL PARKS AND NATURAL WONDERS

Mexico has nearly 60 national parks and biosphere reserves. As the nation's interest in conservation grows, so does its number of parks and reserves. The country is also home to many natural wonders that have not as of yet been declared national parks or reserves.

Popocatepetl and Iztaccihuatl National Park is just outside Mexico City. It is home to the two well-known and well-loved volcanoes, Popo and Izta. Visitors used to climb Popocatepetl. Recently, however, the volcano's rumblings have grown too strong for government officials to allow mountain climbing. Izta is still open for climbing. It stands about 19,000 feet (5,780 meters) in the air. Izta is a challenge to even experienced mountain climbers.

For those visitors to Mexico who would rather swim than climb, the Sea of Cortez is a favorite vacation destination. Mexico's Sea of Cortez has been declared a whale sanctuary, because the waters are the breeding and birthing grounds for gray whales. The whales travel from the Arctic waters of Alaska's Bering Sea to the warm waters off the coast of Baja California. The whales arrive at the Sea of Cortez between December and January, and they stay at least until March but sometimes as late as June.

Mexico has interesting bodies of water *beneath* its ground, as well as along its shores. The *cenotes*, or wells, of the Yucatán are caverns that house underground rivers. These are natural wells, which supplied water to the Yucatán inhabitants of ancient times. The Mayan people treated some cenotes as sacred places. They would come to them to hold religious rites and to make sacrifices.

The beaches of the Yucatán are the nesting grounds for several different species of sea turtles. The loggerhead turtle is one of these species. Kemp's Ridley turtles, another species, follow two major

Mexican folklore refers to Popocatepetl as a great Aztec warrior who was disappointed in love. According to folklore, Popocatépetl and the nearby dormant Iztaccihuatl volcanoes were once star-crossed Aztec lovers. A rumor spread, saying that the warrior had been killed in battle. Hearing these rumors, Iztaccihuatl's father forced her to marry another man. She killed herself in despair. Popocatepetl returned home from battle to find his beloved Iztaccihuatl dead. Overcome with grief, the warrior lifted the woman's dead body and carried her off to the forest where he lay her down gently. The saddened warrior then waited patiently for his love to awaken and come back to him. He is still waiting. This is supposedly why the volcano smokes and rumbles so often. It is the spirit of Popocatepetl bemoaning the death of his love.

"Popocatepetl" means Smoking Mountain in the indigenous Nahuatl language. The residents of Mexico refer to the volcano simply, as "Popo." Popocatepetl is thought to be over 10,000 years old. Hernán Cortés wrote about seeing this mountain erupt in 1519.

Popocatépetl's sister volcano, Ixtaccihuatl, looms over Mexico City in this photograph from the 1920s. The volcanoes and the land surrounding them have been designated a national park by the Mexican government.

The Acapulco beach in Guerrero is one of Mexico's popular resort locations. Mexico's clean white sand beaches are considered some of the most beautiful in the world.

migration routes in the Gulf of Mexico: one northward to the Mississippi area, the other southward to the Campeche Bank, near the Yucatán Peninsula. The green sea turtle is also found in this region.

Every fall, an estimated 250 million Monarch butterflies begin their annual journey to Michoacán, Mexico. This is one of nature's greatest natural phenomena. The orange and black butterflies travel distances of up to 3,100 miles (5,000 kilometers) to avoid the north's winter freezes. From Canada and the United States, the Monarch begins its month-long trip in late October or early November. The butterflies travel more than 70 miles (approximately 112 kilometers) per day. Fortunate viewers can see large groups of butterflies flying overhead. The butterflies fly steadily toward central Mexico's mountaintop pine forests. Their journey ends in the eastern mountains surrounding Morelia, Michoacán's capital. Here in the Oyamel fir forests, the Monarch spends its winter waiting for spring. When springtime finally comes, the butterflies mate. Afterward, they return north. They lay their eggs along their way home.

Located in the Lacandon Rainforest, along the Guatemalan border, is the national park of the Montebello Lakes. There are

The Copper Canyon is in northern Mexico within the state of Chihuahua. It is four times bigger than Arizona's Grand Canyon. The Copper Canyon is almost 300 feet (about 100 meters) deeper than the Grand Canyon.

The Copper Canyon area of Mexico is made up of over 900 miles (1,450 kilometers) of canyons. The canyon system is so large and so deep, that it has mountains within canyons. There are five major canyons in this area.

The Urique River, once a powerful, rushing torrent, carved the main part of the canyon. Today, the Urique River is a small, mild-mannered stream.

Although the trains of the Copper Canyon Railroad also haul timber, it caters mainly to tourists who wish to view this great natural wonder. The Copper Canyon Railroad carries its riders over awe-inspiring chasms, through traditional Tarahumara Indian villages, past rushing rivers, and along alpine forests. The ride from Chihuahua to Los Mochis takes approximately 12 hours. There are 87 tunnels and 35 bridges along the way.

Loggerhead turtles are one of several species that visit Mexico beaches to mate each year. Scientists have equipped this turtle with a satellite transmitter to track its journey.

60 lakes in this park. One of the many groups of lakes in this park is called the Lakes of Colors. The lakes range in color from steel gray and emerald green to amethyst and turquoise. The colors are created by mineral deposits.

Mexico's butterfly-filled forests, beaches covered with nesting sea turtles, mineral-colored lakes, smoldering volcanoes, whale birthing

The annual migration of Monarch butterflies is one of Mexico's unique natural attractions, drawing tourists and nature lovers to Michoacan. The butterflies spend several months in the Mexican forest before returning north.

grounds, and once-sacred underground wells all combine to create a rainbow of national parks and natural wonders. Like a kaleidoscope, Mexico's national parks and natural wonders are constantly changing. They are also, like Mexico, unique and diverse. Mexico's geography is, indeed, an ever-changing kaleidoscope of beauty and diversity.

CHRONOLOGY

10,000 B.C.	Valley of Mexico becomes home to first inhabitants.
9000–1200 B.C.	Corns, beans, and chilies are farmed.
1200–400 B.C.	Rise and fall of Olmec Civilization; the Maya begin their rise.
A.D. 300–900	Mayan culture is at its peak.
900–1000	Toltecs settle in Valley of Mexico.
1325	Aztecs found the city of Tenochtitlán.
1517–1521	Spanish invasion and conquest of Mexico.
1521–1821	Spanish Colonial era of Mexico.
1846–1848	Mexican American War.
1910–1921	Mexican Revolution.
1929	The first formal Mexican political party is born; it is now the Party Revolutionary Institutional, or the PRI.
1943	The Paricutín volcano simultaneously erupts and is born.
1968	Mexico hosts Olympic games.
1985	Earthquake hits Mexico City, killing thousands of people.
1988	Hurricane Gilbert hits Mexico.
1989	Hurricane Hugo causes damage to Cancún, Mexico.
1994	North America Free Trade Agreement between Canada, the United States, and Mexico is signed.
1997	Hurricane Pauline strikes the Pacific coastal states of Guerrero and Oaxaca; tsunamis caused by Hurricane Guillermo flood the Cabos San Lucas area of Mexico.
2000	Vicente Fox elected president.
2002	President Fox meets with other Latin American leaders.

FURTHER READING

Baquedano, Elizabeth. *Eyewitness Books: Aztec, Inca, and Maya*. New York: Knopf, 1993.

Coe, Michael D. *Mexico, From the Olmecs to the Aztecs*. New York: Thames and Hudson, 1997.

Conlon, Laura. *Mexico: The Geography*. Palm Beach, Fla.: Rourke, 1994.

Noble, John. *Mexico*. Oakland, Calif.: Lonely Planet, 2000.

Rand McNally Children's Atlas of Native Americans: Native Cultures of North and South America. Chicago: Rand McNally, 1992.

Sen, Maya. *Let's Go Mexico*. New York: St. Martin's, 2000.

World Factbook. Washington, D.C.: Central Intelligence Agency, 2000.

INTERNET RESOURCES

Facts and figures about Mexico's geography

http://www.mexonline.com/geogrphy.htm
http://www.photius.com/wfb2000/countries/mexico/mexico_geography.html
http://geography.miningco.com/library/maps/blmexico.htm
http://www.theodora.com/gif4/mexico.gif

Information about Mexico

www.nationalgeographic.com/mexico/
www.mexconnect.com
www.elbalero.gob.mx/pages_kids/geography/geography_kids.html

GLOSSARY

Alpine pastures	The mountain slopes above the timberline where low plants grow.
Altitude	Height.
Badland	A region with little plant life.
Basin	A hollow in the surface of the land.
Cacao	The bean used to make chocolate.
Chicle	Sap from the sapodilla tree that is used to make chewing gum.
Coral reefs	Accumulations beneath the ocean of the skeletal remains of a sea creature, which form hard structures.
Ecosystems	A natural community that functions as a unit.
Hydroelectric	Relating to the production of electricity through waterpower.
Mardi Gras	A carnival celebration on the Tuesday before the beginning of Lent, the six weeks of fasting before Easter.
Navigable	Able to be traveled by boats.
Plateau	A high, flat land.
Reservoir	An artificial lake where water is collected and kept for use.
Salsas	Spicy sauces of tomatoes, onions, and peppers.
Serapes	Colorful woolen shawls worn by Mexican women.
Sinkholes	Hollow places where water collects; often connect with an underground cavern or passage.
Sombrero	A wide-brimmed Mexican hat.
Tectonic plates	The large chunks of the earth's crust that sometime shift, creating earthquakes.
Temperate	Mild or moderate temperatures; neither too hot nor too cold.
Tropical	Characteristic of a region or climate that is always frost-free, with temperatures warm enough and enough moisture to support year-round plant life.
Tsunamis	Tidal waves.

INDEX

63

PICTURE CREDITS

CONTRIBUTORS

Roger E. Hernández is the most widely syndicated columnist writing on Hispanic issues in the United States. His weekly column, distributed by King Features, appears in some 40 newspapers across the country, including the *Washington Post*, *Los Angeles Daily News*, *Dallas Morning News*, *Arizona Republic*, *Rocky Mountain News* in Denver, *El Paso Times*, and *Hartford Courant*. He is also the author of *Cubans in America*, an illustrated history of the Cuban presence in what is now the United States, from the early colonists in 16th-century Florida to today's Castro-era exiles. The book was designed to accompany a PBS documentary of the same title.

Hernández's articles and essays have been published in the *New York Times*, *New Jersey Monthly*, *Reader's Digest*, and *Vista Magazine*; he is a frequent guest on television and radio political talk shows, and often travels the country to lecture on his topic of expertise. Currently, he is teaching journalism and English composition at the New Jersey Institute of Technology in Newark, where he holds the position of writer-in-residence. He is also a member of the adjunct faculty at Rutgers University.

Hernández left Cuba with his parents at the age of nine. After living in Spain for a year, the family settled in Union City, New Jersey, where Hernandez grew up. He attended Rutgers University, where he earned a BA in Journalism in 1977; after graduation, he worked in television news before moving to print journalism in 1983. He lives with his wife and two children in Upper Montclair, New Jersey.

Colleen Madonna Flood Williams holds a bachelor's degree in elementary education, with a minor in art. She is the author of numerous study units, magazine articles, newspaper articles, essays, and poems. Colleen lives in Soldotna, Alaska, with her husband Paul, her son Dillon, and their Bouvier des Flandres dog, Kosmos Kramer.